Victorian Christmas Cookbook and Traditions

By

The Chiappa Sisters

form of brain injury caused by sudden damage to the brain. (I got mine from having two strokes) I share this with you not to gain your sympathy but to share and inspire that people with disabilities can do anything they set their mind to.

Table of Contents

For   Anthony, My one and only.

Christmas is a special time a year. The time of year that the World slows down, when people smile at strangers, and Peace reigns on Earth. What would the Christmas season be without tasty food?

Many of today's Christmas traditions and recipes originated from Victorian England.

In this book, you will read about favorite customs family and friends shared during the Christmas season in Victorian times, including the customs of Christmas crackers, advent wreath, how Boxing Day got started, Christmas Cards and many others.

Treat your family to some of the mouth-watering recipes in this book including,

Honey Glazed Carrots and Parsnips, Champagne Punch, Victorian Eggnog, Chocolate Chip Zucchini Bread, English Toffee, Spicy Roast Turkey

Boxing Day Festive Roast Pumpkin and Cheese Lasagna, Chocolate Dipped Krispies Peanut Butter Balls Chunky Apple Spice Cake With Vanilla Butter Sauce, Spiced Cranberry Sauce, Pistachio Pudding Supreme, Green Beans With Lemon and Almonds, Cranberry Orange Quick Bread, Apricot-Glazed Roasted Asparagus, Stuffed Celery, Cranberry Spice Tea, Fresh Orange Slices with Honey and Cinnamon, Cranberry Sage Stuffing, Sweet Potato Casserole w/Coconut Pecan topping, and many others!

The History of Christmas

It's hard to imagine now, but at the beginning of the 19th century Christmas was hardly celebrated. Many businesses did not even consider it a holiday. However, by the end of the century it had become the biggest annual celebration and took on the form that we recognize today.

The transformation happened quickly, and came from all sectors of society.

Many attributes the change to Queen Victoria, and it was her marriage to the German-born Prince Albert that introduced some of the most prominent aspects of Christmas. In 1848 the Illustrated London News published a drawing of the royal family celebrating around a decorated Christmas tree, a tradition that was reminiscent of Prince Albert's childhood in Germany. Soon every home in Britain had a tree bedecked with candles, sweets, fruit, homemade decorations and small gifts.

In 1843 Henry Cole commissioned an artist to design a card for Christmas. The illustration showed a group of people around a dinner table and a Christmas message. At one shilling each, these were pricey for ordinary Victorians and so were not immediately accessible. However, the sentiment caught on and many children - Queen Victoria's included – were encouraged to make their own Christmas cards. In this age of industrialization color printing technology quickly became more advanced, causing the price of card production to drop significantly. Together with the introduction of the halfpenny postage rate, the Christmas card industry took off. By the 1880s the sending of cards had become hugely popular, creating a lucrative industry that produced 11.5 million cards in 1880 alone. The commercialization of Christmas was well on its way.

Another commercial Christmas industry was borne by Victorians in 1848 when a British confectioner, Tom Smith, invented a bold new way to sell sweets. Inspired by a trip to Paris where he saw bon bons – sugared almonds wrapped in twists of paper – he came up with the idea of the Christmas cracker: a simple package filled with sweets that snapped when pulled apart. The sweets were replaced by small gifts and paper hats in the late Victorian period, and remain in this form as an essential part of a modern Christmas.

Decorating the home at Christmas also became a more elaborate affair. The medieval tradition of using evergreens continued, however the style and placement of these decorations became more important. The custom of simply decking walls and windows with sprigs and twigs was sniffed at. Uniformity, order and elegance were encouraged. There were instructions on how to make elaborate synthetic decorations for those residing in towns. In 1881 Casswell's Family Magazine gave strict directions to the lady of the house: "To bring about a general feeling of enjoyment, much depends on the surroundings... It is worthwhile to bestow some little trouble on the decoration of the rooms".

Gift giving had traditionally been at New Year but moved as Christmas became more important to the Victorians. Initially gifts were rather modest – fruit, nuts, sweets and small handmade trinkets. These were usually hung on the Christmas tree. However, as gift giving became more central to the festival, and the gifts became bigger and shop-bought, they moved under the tree. The Christmas feast has its roots from before the Middle Ages, but it's during the Victorian period that the dinner we now associate with Christmas began to take shape. Examination of early Victorian recipes shows that mince pies were initially made from meat, a tradition dating back to Tudor times. However, during the 19th century there was a revolution in the composition of this festive dish. Mixes without meat began to gain popularity within some of the higher echelons of society and became the mince pies we know today.

The roast turkey also has its beginnings in Victorian Britain. Previously other forms of roasted meat such as beef and goose were the centerpiece of the Christmas dinner. The turkey was added to this by the wealthier sections of the community in the 19th century, but its perfect size for a middle class family gathering meant it became the dominant dish by the beginning of the 20th century.

While carols were not new to the Victorians, it was a tradition that they actively revived and popularized. The Victorians considered carols to be a delightful form of musical entertainment, and a pleasure well worth cultivating. Old words were put to new tunes and the first significant collection of carols was published in 1833 for all to enjoy.

The Victorians also transformed the idea of Christmas so that it became centered around the family. The preparation and eating of the feast, decorations and gift giving, entertainments and parlor games - all were essential to the celebration of the festival and were to be shared by the whole family.

While Charles Dickens did not invent the Victorian Christmas, his book A Christmas Carol is credited with helping to popularize and spread the traditions of the festival. Its themes of family, charity, goodwill, peace and happiness encapsulate the spirit of the Victorian Christmas, and are very much a part of the Christmas we celebrate today.

times, young ladies spent many hours making Christmas decorations. They made little horns of plenty from colored paper which could be filled with dates or other sweets; from small pieces of silk and feathers, they created little pouches and bags for candied fruits and almonds; from silk threads or ribbons elaborate pompons (tassels) were produced and they used cotton wool to make little snowmen or cute angels.

St. Stephens Day (December 26), Boxing Day

The first day after the Christmas festivities is devoted to charity. Small money gifts are packed in boxes and given to servants, delivery people or the local needy. This is the origin of the name "Boxing Day". Charity was a duty for the well-to-do and the upper class of Victorian society and was rigorously observed.

Games were also played here are a few, you might enjoy playing with your own family:

The Laughing Game:

1. All players sit in a circle

2. Each player takes it in turns to say "Ha", "Ho" or "Hee".

3. The first player to start laughing loses and is out of the game.

4. Continue until everyone is out of the game.

5. The person who manages not to laugh for the longest is the winner.

The Sculptor

1. Choose one player to be The Sculptor.

2. All other players stand in a still position.

3. The Sculptor must then move the other players into strange poses that are difficult to hold.

. The other players must not laugh, break pose or move.

5. The Sculptor can distract the other players and encourage them to laugh, but they must not touch them.

6. The first player to move or laugh, loses and becomes The Sculptor.

Make Your Own Victorian Keepsake Box.

Items Needed

Box

Newspaper cuts into strips

Glue

Scissors

Paint

Items to decorate

Step-by-Step Instructions

To make the box you can download the template and instructions. Or you might already have a box that you would like to use.

Step 1: Cover a box with newspaper soaked in glue

Add some water to PVA glue in a bowl. For thick glues the ratio is usually 50:50. The paste needs to be slightly watered down, but not too runny. You could also use 1 part flour to 5 parts water and boil for about 3 minutes.

Rip or cut the newspaper into small strips. Take one piece, soak it in the glue mix, and then gently place onto the box. Repeat this with another strip of paper, laying this one slightly over-lapping the previous strip.

Continue to do this until the whole box is covered, ensuring that you have covered the edges.

Cover the box lid in the same way. Leave to dry overnight and then apply another layer. You can repeat this if necessary.

Step 2: Paint and decorate the box

You can decorate your box in any way you like. We chose to paint our box using black, as Japanese style lacquer was a popular aesthetic in Victorian times. Apply paint thinly, but make sure you cover the whole outside and inside of the box. Place to one side whilst you wait for the paint to dry. You can apply another coat if necessary.

Gather together your items for decorating the box. You could use dried flowers or leaves and stick them onto you box in an attractive pattern, or maybe you would like to use buttons or shells. It doesn't matter what you use, the important part is making the box look as special and lavish as possible.

Now the box is finished it will make a great gift for someone to keep special items in like a necklace.

Make Your Own Victorian Mistletoe Ball

Victorians made mistletoe balls for the same reason we hang mistletoe today, to steal a kiss from an unsuspecting person passing under it. The mistletoe ball or 'kissing ball' was always made out of evergreen branches and was often decorated with scented herbs and foliage.

Items Needed

Wire or thin cane

Mistletoe

Greenery - holly, ivy

Ribbon

Scissors

Items to decorate

Step 1: Make two circles from wire and tie together

Bend a piece of wire or thin cane into a circle and bind the ends together with string. Do this again, so you now have two circles.

To make the frame, place the two circles together, making a globe like structure. Bind the two wire circles together with string at all conjoining edges.

Step 2: Wind greenery around the frame.

Cover the wire frame with all kinds of festive greenery, like holly, ivy and yew. Weave the branches around each other and the wire frame.

Step 3: Add decorations

Decorate

Attach other items like dried roses and holly berries with wire.

Step 4: Suspend the mistletoe using ribbon

Attach the mistletoe

Tie some ribbon in a loop at the top of the newly decorated ball ready for hanging. Add a length of ribbon to the bottom of ball and tie a sprig of mistletoe to it.

Step 5: Hang the mistletoe kissing ball

Hang the mistletoe ball

Hang the mistletoe ball above a door or in a walkway and wait beneath it until someone comes along to give you a kiss.

Make Your Own Victorian Paper Flowers

Victorians loved the aesthetic of paper flowers as decorations. There are hundreds of articles from the magazines of the time showing how to make different types of flowers. Most were highly elaborate designs, but we've found a simple rose flower for your first go.

Items Needed

Colored Paper

Green crepe paper

Florist wire

Glue

Scissors

Step 1: Fold the paper into four and cut out the petals

Fold the petals

Take a colored piece of paper and fold into four. Draw on the shape from the template, or simply cut out a heart shape.

Step 2: Score the petals

Score the petals

Score the petals using a spoon or your nail to give it shape and movement.

Step 3: Build up the petals to create the rose flower

Build up the rose flower

Create the flower by rolling one of the petals into a tight cone. Take another petal, and place it where the first roll ends. Pinch the bottom tightly to secure them in place. After about four pieces start attaching the petals the other way around, so they face outwards.

Step 4: Use wire to hold the petals and create the stem

Use florist wire to create the stem

Take a piece of florist wire and wrap it tightly around the base of the flower, then extend it, making the rest into the stem.

Step 5: Twist crepe paper around the wire

Twist crepe paper around the wire

Cut strips of green crepe paper. Glue the end onto the top of the stem at the base of the flower, and then tightly wrap the rest of the paper around the length of the wire.

You can make multiple flowers to create a bouquet of paper flowers.

Victorian Eggnog

Ingredients:

2 cups whipping cream

1 cup half-and-half

6 large egg yolks

1/2cup sugar

1 teaspoon nutmeg

6 tablespoons dry sherry

additional ground nutmeg

Directions

Bring cream and half and half to simmer in large saucepan. Whisk yolks and sugar in large bowl to blend. Gradually whisk hot cream mixture into yolk mixture. Return mixture to same saucepan. Stir over medium-low heat until mixture thickens and leaves path on back of spoon when finger is drawn across, about 4 minutes (do not boil). Strain into bowl. Stir in nutmeg. Cool slightly. (Can be made 1 day ahead, Cover and chill. If desired, rewarm over low heat stirring occasionally, before continuing).

Divide warm or cold mixture amount 6 cups or glasses. Stir 1 tablespoon sherry into each. Sprinkle additional nutmeg over each and serve.

Chocolate Chip Zucchini Bread

Ingredients:

6 eggs

4 cups sugar

2 cups oil

4 -5 cups zucchini, shredded

6 cups flour

2 teaspoons baking soda

1 teaspoon baking powder

2 teaspoons salt

1 tablespoon cinnamon

1 tablespoon vanilla

1(12 ounce) package miniature chocolate chips

Directions

Preheat oven to 325 degrees.

Beat together eggs, sugar and oil.

Add zucchini and remaining ingredients, mixing well.

Bake in 4 well-greased loaf pans for about one hour.

Chocolate Chip Zucchini Bread

English Toffee

Ingredients:

1 cup butter (only real butter can be used in this recipe)

1 cup sugar

1/4 cup water

1/2 teaspoon salt

3 semi-sweet chocolate baking squares or 1/2 cup chocolate chips

1 cup coarsely broken pecans

Directions

In heavy saucepan, combine butter, sugar, water, and salt.

Cook to hard-crack stage (300°F) stirring with a WOODEN SPOON constantly and watching carefully. Do not try a plastic spoon, it will melt into your delicious candy!

Immediately pour into ungreased 13"x9" pan.

Cool until hard.

Melt chocolate over hot, but not boiling water.

Spread over toffee; sprinkle with nuts, pressing them into chocolate.

Let stand 2-3 hours or chill 30 minutes.

Break into bite-size pieces.

English Toffee

Spicy Roast Turkey

Ingredients:

1 -1 1/2cup mayonnaise

2 tablespoons paprika

1/2teaspoon cayenne pepper

1/2teaspoon black pepper

2 teaspoons salt

1 teaspoon onion powder

1 teaspoon oregano

1 teaspoon thyme

1 teaspoon garlic powder

1(14 lb) turkey

Directions

Mix the spices into the mayonnaise until thoroughly blended.

Tuck back the wings and slather the spicy paste all over the turkey, massaging it into the bird.

(Rub inside the bird, outside the bird and make sure to spread it under the breast skin).

Roast on lowest rack of the oven at 500°F for 30 minutes.

Remove the turkey from the oven and cover the breast with a double layer of heavy duty aluminum foil folded into a triangle (leaving the legs and dark meat uncovered), insert a thermometer into thickest part of the breast and return it to oven.

Reduce the oven temperature to 350°F.

Roast until the turkey temperature reaches 161°F (14 to 16 pound bird only needs a total of 2 to 2 1/2 hours of roasting).

Remove the turkey from the oven and let it rest, loosely covered for at least 15 minutes before carving.

Spicy Roast Turkey

Boxing Day Festive Roast Pumpkin and Cheese Lasagne

Ingredients:

PUMPKIN FILLING

2 tablespoons olive oil

30 g unsalted butter

8 sage leaves

2 onions, peeled and finely chopped

3 garlic cloves, peeled and minced

2 1/4kg pumpkin, peeled, deseeded and cut into 3cm rough cubes

5 ml vermouth or 5 ml white wine

60 ml water

1(400 g) can chopped tomatoes

salt & freshly ground black pepper

TOMATO SAUCE

2(400 g) cans chopped tomatoes

500 ml water

2 tablespoons sugar

1 tablespoon sea salt or 1 teaspoon table salt

good grinding pepper

CHEESE LAYER

225g soft fresh goat's cheese

225 g cream cheese with garlic and herbs

250 g grated cheddar cheese

500 g ricotta cheese

3 large organic eggs

good grating fresh nutmeg

LASAGNE

2(300 g) packetsfresh lasagna sheets,
600g total

2 balls mozzarella cheese

125 g pine nuts, toasted

salt and pepper

Directions

Preheat the oven to 200C/180C
fan/400F/gas 6, slipping in a baking
sheet as you do.

To make the pumpkin filling: heat the
oil and butter in a shallow casserole
dish or roasting tin and fry the sage
leaves over a gentle heat for about 2
minutes. Add the chopped onion and
minced garlic to the pan and fry very
gently for another 10 minutes or so.
Add the pumpkin pieces, turn well in
the oniony oil and then add the

vermouth (or wine), the water and chopped tomatoes. Roast in a pre-heated oven for 30 to 45 minutes, stirring occasionally. Taste for seasoning – I tend to add quite a bit of salt here – and leave to cool.

For the tomato sauce: simply pour the chopped tomatoes and water into a large jug or bowl, and stir in the sugar, salt and pepper, whisking it all together.

To make up the cheese layer: in a separate bowl beat the goat's cheese, cream cheese, Cheddar and ricotta with the eggs, nutmeg, and salt and pepper to taste.

To assemble the lasagne, begin by putting 500ml of the cold tomato sauce in the bottom of a roasting tin (measuring approx 36cm x 26cm x 6cm). Then layer with a third of the lasagne sheets, overlapping them well. Leave the rest of the tomato sauce aside for the time being.

Layer a third of the pumpkin filling over the lasagne, and dollop on a third of the cheese mixture, coaxing with a rubber spatula. It won't cover completely; think more of spreading blobs about. Then start again with a layer of lasagne, followed by pumpkin, then the cheese. Repeat once more – lasagne, pumpkin, and the last of the cheese mixture. Pour the remaining cold tomato sauce over, letting it sink down and be absorbed in the layers.

Slice and chop the mozzarella balls and dot over the top.

Cook in the oven, on the baking sheet, for 1 hour. Once cooked, take out of the oven and let it stand for 15-30 minutes to make cutting and serving easier. (I love this when it's been standing for an hour or so, too.) As you cut and slice, you will notice a shallow tomatoey cheesy pool at the bottom of the tin; bread dunked into this is gorgeous.

Sprinkle the toasted pine nuts over the lasagne, and cut into squares to serve.

MAKE AHEAD TIP Up to 2 days ahead, make the pumpkin filling, leave to cool and keep, covered, in the fridge. Make the cheese layer and keep, covered, in the fridge. When ready to use, assemble the lasagne and cook as directed.

FREEZE AHEAD TIP Cook, cool and freeze the cooked pumpkin for up to 1 week. Thaw overnight in the fridge. When ready to use, assemble the lasagne and cook as directed.

Boxing Day Festive Roast Pumpkin and Cheese Lasagne

Chocolate Dipped Krispies Peanut Butter Balls

Ingredients:

1cup butter or 1/2 cup margarine

2 cups chunky peanut butter

1 teaspoon vanilla (optional)

1 lb powdered sugar

3cups rice, krispies

Chocolate Dip

2 ounces paraffin wax or 2 ounces shortening

1(24 ounce) package chocolate chips (using 12 ounces for large balls or 24 ounces for small one)

Directions

Melt butter and while hot, stir in peanut butter.

Mix well and add vanilla, powdered sugar and Rice Krispies.

Work in with hands until it will form balls.

If using paraffin shred on a box grater then add to the chocolate in a double boil and heat till melted and combined.

Dip into melted chocolate and paraffin or shortening with toothpick.

Cool on waxed paper.

Chocolate Dipped Krispies Peanut Butter Balls

Chunky Apple Spice Cake with Vanilla Butter Sauce

Ingredients:

1/2cup butter, softened

1 cup firmly packed light brown sugar

2 eggs

2 teaspoons pure vanilla extract

1 cup all-purpose flour

1tablespoon pumpkin pie spice

1 teaspoon ground allspice

1⁄teaspoon salt

2 cups peeled and chopped apples (Granny Smith or Gala)

1/2cup chopped walnuts

1/2cup raisins (optional)

1 1/2teaspoons baking powder

Vanilla Butter Sauce

1⁄2cup butter

1⁄2cup whipping cream

1 cup firmly packed light brown sugar

2 tablespoons pure vanilla extract

Directions

Preheat oven to 350°F degrees.

Beat butter and brown sugar for 5 minutes in a mixer bowl.

Beat in eggs and vanilla just until blended.

Set aside.

Mix flour, pumpkin pie spice, baking powder, allspice and salt.

Gradually add to sugar mixture; beating until well blended.

Stir in apples, nuts, and raisins, if desired.

Pour into one greased 9-inch baking pan; bake 35-40 minutes or until toothpick inserted in center comes out clean.

Cool on wire rack 10 minutes.

Serve warm with Vanilla Butter Sauce.

Vanilla Butter Sauce:.

Combine butter and whipping cream with brown sugar.

Bring to boil over medium heat.

Reduce heat; simmer 10 minutes or until slightly thickened.

Remove from heat; stir in vanilla.

Serve warm.

Do-ahead Suggestion: The cake and sauce can be prepared and refrigerated separately the day before.

Warm the cake, in the oven, and the sauce, on top of the stove, before serving.

Chunky Apple Spice Cake with Vanilla Butter Sauce

Champagne Punch

Ingredients:

1(12 ounce) can frozen lemonade concentrate, thawed (small can)

1(12 ounce) can frozen orange juice concentrate, thawed (small can)

1(12 ounce) can frozen limeade concentrate, thawed (may use 1 small can pineapple juice concentrate, thawed)

1(2 liter) bottle ginger ale, chilled

1(2 liter) bottle champagne, chilled

Directions

Mix the juice concentrates in punch bowl (do not add water).

Stir in the Gingerale then add the Champagne (do not stir after adding the champagne!)

Champagne Punch

Honey Glazed Carrots and Parsnips

Ingredients:

1 cup vegetable broth or 1 cup water (adding more if needed)

1 lb. carrot, peeled and cut into 1/4-inch pieces on an angle

1 lb. parsnip, peeled and cut into 1/4-inch pieces on an angle

1 tablespoon unsalted butter

1 teaspoon honey

1 small onion, sliced thinly

salt and pepper, to taste

Directions

In a pot boil broth, cook the carrots and parsnips in the broth for 10 to 15 minutes, or until they are just tender, and transfer them to a bowl.

In a skillet melt the butter and sauté onions till tender add honey. If carrots and parsnips aren't sweet you can add more honey.

Add the carrots and parsnips, Cook the mixture over moderately low heat, stirring, for 1 to 2 minutes, or until the carrots and parsnips are glazed evenly and heated through, and season it with salt and pepper.

Honey Glazed Carrots and Parsnips

Spiced Cranberry Sauce

Ingredients:

1(12 ounce) bag cranberries

1/2cup honey

2 -3 tablespoons firmly packed brown sugar (or to taste)

2 cinnamon sticks (3-inch)

6 whole cloves

1/4teaspoon freshly grated nutmeg (or to taste)

3/4cup water (I use orange juice instead of water)

Directions

Combine all ingredients in a saucepan and simmer, covered, stirring occasionally for 5 to 10 minutes, or until the cranberries have burst and the mixture has thickened. (I put the cloves in a tea diffuser for easier removal and usually cook the sauce a little longer than the time given.).

Transfer the sauce to a bowl and let cool.

The sauce may be made 2 days in advance and kept covered and chilled.

Serve at room temperature.

Spiced Cranberry Sauce

Pistachio Pudding Supreme

Ingredients:

1(8 ounce) container Cool Whip

1(8 ounce) package cream cheese, softened

1(8 ounce) can pineapple, crushed

1 cup walnuts, chopped

2 cups colored miniature marshmallows

2(3 ounce) boxes instant pistachio pudding mix

Directions

Mix all ingredients in a large serving bowl, until well combined.

Refrigerate for 1 hour before serving.

Pistachio Pudding Supreme

Green Beans With Lemon and Almonds

Ingredients:

2 lbs fresh green beans, trimmed

7 tablespoons butter (can use a bit less)

1 cup almonds, coarsley chopped (or sliced)

1 tablespoon minced lemon peel (use the yellow part only, can use a bit more lemon peel)

1/3cup finely chopped parsley

salt and pepper

Directions

Cook the green beans in a pot with salted water until JUST tender (about 5 minutes, you can steam the also) drain and transfer to a large bowl of ice water to cool; drain and pat dry with a paper towel (this can be done a day ahead).

Melt butter in a skillet over medium heat.

Add in chopped almonds, and toss with butter; saute the nuts until they are lightly browned and crisp (about 2-3 minutes).

Add in beans, and toss to combine with the nuts until heated through (about 3-4 minutes).

Mix in the lemon peel; cook 1 minute.

Mix in the chopped parsley.

Season with salt and pepper, and transfer to a bowl.

Green Beans With Lemon and Almonds

Cranberry Orange Quick Bread

Ingredients:

2 cups all-purpose flour

3/4 cup sugar

2 teaspoons baking powder

1/2 teaspoon baking soda

1 teaspoon salt

1/4 cup butter (shortening)

3/4 cup orange juice

1 tablespoon grated orange rind

2 eggs, well beaten

1 cup coarsely chopped cranberries, leave a few whole

1/2 cup chopped glace green cherries (optional)

Directions

Stir flour, sugar, baking powder, baking soda and salt together.

Cut in butter until mixture resembles coarse cornmeal.

Combine orange juice and grated rind with well beaten eggs.

Pour all at once into dry ingredients, mixing just enough to dampen.

Dust chopped cranberries and cherries with a tablespoon of flour, carefully fold into batter Spoon into a well buttered 1 1/2 quart casserole.

Sprinkle a few floured whole cranberries over top of batter.

Bake in a moderate oven, 350 degrees about 1 hour or until toothpick inserted in centre comes out clean.

Cool in casserole 10 minutes, then remove.

Store overnight for easy slicing.

Frost with confectioner's frosting, (sift 2 cups icing sugar, very slowly add boiling water, a tablespoon at a time, until right spreading consistency, spread on slightly cooled bread).

Also delicious sliced with butter or toasted under broiler, spread with butter and sprinkled with cheddar.

Cranberry Orange Quick Bread

Apricot-Glazed Roasted Asparagus

Ingredients:

1 lb fresh asparagus spear (ends trimmed)

3 tablespoons apricot preserves

1 tablespoon soy sauce

1/8-1/teaspoon garlic powder

1/4teaspoon salt

black pepper

Directions

Rinse spears under cold water then pat dry with paper towels.

Set oven to 375 degrees.

Grease a large baking sheet.

In a small bowl combine the apricot preserves with soy sauce, garlic powder and salt; pour over the asparagus on the baking sheet and toss using hands to coat with the mixture.

Bake for about 10-15 minutes or until the asparagus is crisp-tender.

Season with freshly ground black pepper to taste.

Apricot-Glazed Roasted Asparagus

Stuffed Celery

Ingredients:

1 bunch celery

1(8 ounce) package cream cheese (I use reduced fat)

2 tablespoons sour cream (I use light)

1/4cup chopped walnuts

20 small green olives

Directions

Coarsely chop the olives. Separate and wash celery stalks. Can remove celery strings, if desired.

Mix cream cheese and sour cream. Stir in walnuts and olives.

Spread filling into celery. Cut into bite-sized pieces. Chill until serving time.

Stuffed Celery

Cranberry Spice Tea

Ingredients:

3 cups tea, brewed

3 cups cranberry juice cocktail

2 tablespoons sugar

3 cinnamon sticks

Directions

Heat all ingredients to boiling; reduce heat.

Simmer uncovered 20 minutes, stirring occasionally.

Remove cinnamon sticks.

Serve tea warm.

Cranberry Spice Tea

Fresh Orange Slices with Honey and Cinnamon

Ingredients:

4 oranges

3 tablespoons honey

1 cinnamon stick

1 tablespoon orange flower water

3 tablespoons sliced almonds, lightly toasted

thick Greek yogurt or sour cream (optional)

Directions

Using small sharp knife, cut off peel and white pith from oranges.

Thinly slice oranges into rounds.

Arrange orange slices in shallow bowl.

Combine honey, cinnamon stick, and orange flower water in heavy small saucepan.

Stir over low heat until mixture comes to simmer, about 2 minutes.

Pour hot syrup over oranges.

Cool.

(Can be prepared 1 day ahead. Cover and chill.) Sprinkle almonds over oranges.

Serve cold or at room temperature, with a dollop of yoghurt or sour cream on the side, if desired

Fresh Orange Slices with Honey and Cinnamon

Cranberry Sage Stuffing

Ingredients:

6 tablespoons butter

1 cup chopped onion

1 cup chopped celery (use leaves too well chopped)

2 cups chopped cranberries, fresh frozen or dried

4 cups white bread, cubes crusts removed

2 teaspoons fresh sage or 1/2 teaspoon dried sage

1 orange, rind of, grated

2 tablespoons brown sugar or 2 tablespoons brown sugar substitute

2 eggs, lightly beaten

salt & pepper

1 cup chicken stock

Directions

In a large skillet melt the butter, do not brown, and add the onions- saute for 3 minutes then add the celery, stir.

Continue adding one ingredient at a time until all the ingredients are in the pan Stir lightly after each addition.

Turn into an oiled oven proof dish.

You may now refrigerate it covered until the next day or.

Bake in 350F oven for 30 minutes it should be nicely browned and cooked through.

Cranberry Sage Stuffing

Sweet Potato Casserole w/Coconut Pecan topping

Ingredients:

Casserole

4 cups mashed sweet potatoes

1/4 cup sugar

1 teaspoon vanilla

1/2 cup half-and-half

2 eggs, beaten

salt

Topping

1 cup coconut

1/3 cup brown sugar

1 cup chopped pecans

1/3 cup flour

1/3 cup melted butter

Directions

Mix all of the casserole ingredients in a mixer until smooth, then spread in a buttered dish.

Mix well topping ingredients and add melted butter.

Sprinkle on top of the potatoes.

Bake at 375 for 25 minutes.

Sweet Potato Casserole w/Coconut Pecan topping

Crab Artichoke and Spinach Dip

Ingredients:

1(8 ounce) package cream cheese, room temp

8 ounces imitation crabmeat, chopped

1(4 ounce) jar artichokes, chopped

1 cup parmesan cheese, shredded

1 cup mayonnaise

1 box frozen spinach, thawed

Directions

Put spinach into colander and press out excess liquid.

Mix all together into a small crockpot and let bake for at least 1 hour on low.

Serve with tortilla chips, or bagel chips, or spread on baguettes.

Crab Artichoke and Spinach Dip

Squash With Apple Cider and Herb Glaze

Ingredients:

2 lbs acorn squash or 2 lbs butternut squash or 2 lbs winter squash, weight approximate

1 1/2cups apple juice or 1 1/2 cups apple cider

1 cup water

2 teaspoons apple cider vinegar

salt & freshly ground black pepper, to taste

Herb Butter

3 tablespoons unsalted butter

1/4cup fresh sage, coarsely chopped or 1/4 cup about 1 1/2 tbsp ground sage

1 tablespoon fresh rosemary, coarsely chopped or 1 teaspoon dried rosemary

1 teaspoon cinnamon, preferably freshly grated

1/4 teaspoon nutmeg, preferably freshly grated

Directions

Peel squash and seed it. Cut squash into cubes 1 inch wide by 1/2 inch thick.

Melt butter in a 12 inch skillet over medium to medium low heat.

Add sage and rosemary and cook, stirring until the butter just begins to turn golden brown. Do not brown the herbs. Stir in the cinnamon and nutmeg.

Add the squash to the skillet, then the juice, water, vinegar and a pinch of salt.

Bring the mixture to a boil, increasing the heat if need be. Reduce heat and keep it at a simmer.

Stir occasionally until the juice has boiled down to a glaze and the squash is as tender as you want it. Time varies with type of squash. It takes about 45 minutes to 1 hour.

Taste and season with salt and pepper.

Serve.

Squash With Apple Cider and Herb Glaze

Winter Wassail

Ingredients:

1 gallon apple cider

1 tablespoon whole cloves

1 tablespoon whole allspice

4 cinnamon sticks, 2-inch long

1/2 teaspoon mace

1/4 teaspoon powdered ginger

14/teaspoon grated nutmeg

1/4 teaspoon salt

1 cup dark brown sugar

1 pint gin (optional) or 1 pint vodka, this is (optional)

2 lemons, sliced thin, seeds removed

3 oranges, sliced thin, seeds removed

Directions

Pour cider into large kettle, add spices and salt. Bring to a hard boil, reduce heat and simmer 15 minutes

Remove from stove, add sugar to taste, if needed.

Cool. Strain wassail. Keep in a cool place till ready to use, but it is not necessary to refrigerate.

To prepare a wassail bowl: Use a heavy china bowl, a crock pot or a punch bowl.

Heat it over a large kettle of boiling water. Add lemon and orange slices.

When warm, add gin or vodka and let it heat, but do not boil or spirits will evaporate. Remove from heat.

Pour in the boiling wassail. If possible keep the bowl hot over a candle or alcohol burner. Ladle into punch cups and serve.

Winter Wassail

Candy Cane Hot White Chocolate

Ingredients:

12 cups milk

9 ounces white chocolate, chopped

1 cup crushed candy canes or 1 cup hard peppermint candy

1/4 teaspoon salt

1 1/2 cups peppermint schnapps

whipped cream

additional crushed peppermint candy

Directions

In a large saucepan, heat milk and bring to a simmer.

Add white chocolate, 1 cup candy, and salt.

Whisk mixture until smooth.

Add schnapps and mix until heated through.

Ladle mixture into mugs.

Top with whipped cream and crushed peppermints.

Candy Cane Hot White Chocolate

Chocolate Coffee Kiss

Ingredients:

1ounce coffee liqueur

3/4ounce Irish cream

1/2ounce Creme de Cacao (dark)

1 teaspoon Grand Marnier (or other brandy-based orange liqueur)

1 1/2ounces chocolate syrup

1 cup coffee (hot, freshly brewed)

whipped cream

1 maraschino cherries (garnish) or 1 chocolate shavings (garnish)

Directions

In an Irish coffee mug, combine coffee liqueur, Irish cream, creme de cacao and Grand Marnier. Add half of the chocolate syrup, then fill mug with hot coffee; stir gently.

Top with a dollop of whipped cream, drizzle with remaining chocolate syrup and garnish with a maraschino cherry or a few chocolate shavings.

Chocolate Coffee Kiss

Stuffed Roast Duck with Balsamic Cherry Sauce

Ingredients:

1(6 lb) duck (approx)

salt

garlic pepper seasoning

4 1/2cups cooked brown rice

1 cup chopped onion

7 -8 sprigs fresh sage, chopped

6 tablespoons sweet butter (also called unsalted)

3/4cup chopped pecans

1 teaspoon salt

1(15 ounce) canpitted cherries, drained

2 cups red wine

1/2cup honey

½ cup balsamic vinegar

Directions

Preheat oven to 375ºF.

To prepare the stuffing: Sauté onion in butter until onion is transparent.

Remove from heat.

In a large bowl Add salt, and combine with rice, chopped sage and pecans.

Taste and adjust seasoning to your taste.

You may wish to add more salt and if you like you can add a bit of garlic pepper, but that is optional.

Remove the bag from the duck cavity that contains the giblets and neck bone and set aside in refrigerator, you won't need it for this recipe.

Rinse and dry the duck.

Stuff the duck with the prepared brown rice stuffing and sew the stuffed cavity closed or secure with round tooth picks.

Place the stuffed duck on a rack in a roasting pan breast side up and sprinkle all over top and bottom with salt and garlic pepper.

Ducks contain lots of natural fat so require no basting.

Roast at 375ºF for about 22 minutes a pound.

A 6 pound duck should be done in about 2 1/4 hours.

When duck is done let it set for about 20 minutes to let the juices settle before carving.

While the duck is resting prepare the cherry sauce: In a medium size saucepan, combine the 15 ounce can of cherries, honey, wine, and Balsamic vinegar.

Heat over medium flame until the mixture is reduced by half.

Transfer to a serving touraine with a ladle.

Place the touraine on table beside the carved Duck and let guests spoon as much sauce as they like on their portion of duck.

Stuffed Roast Duck with Balsamic Cherry Sauce

Have a merry Christmas!

Printed in Great Britain
by Amazon

14718871R00068